Guide to Modern Personal Finance: For Students and Young Adults

Guide to Modern Personal Finance, Volume 1

Matthew Green

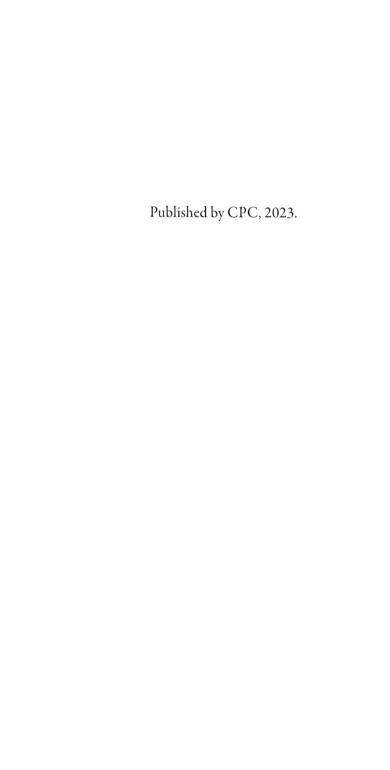

Published by CPC, 2023.

While every precaution has been taken in the preparation of this book, the publisher assumes no responsibility for errors or omissions, or for damages resulting from the use of the information contained herein.

GUIDE TO MODERN PERSONAL FINANCE: FOR STUDENTS AND YOUNG ADULTS

First edition. May 8, 2023.

Written by Matthew Green.

Guide to Modern Personal Finance:

For Students and Young Adults

By Matthew Green

Preface

This book contains the culmination of decades of experience including timeless advice given to me and those learned through experiences working in finance, tech, law, and education. Financial advice is inherently conservative, so these guidelines will not fit every person's lifestyle, goals, and most importantly relation to risk aversion. As you read this book, critically consider how you may apply and incorporate these lessons into your life in a sustainable way that also allows you to reach your financial goals. With a bit of knowledge, diligence, and hard work, you can achieve the financial future of your dreams.

Good luck on your endeavors– your wealth awaits!

"An investment in knowledge always pays the best interest."

~Benjamin Franklin

Part 1: Borrowing Money

Loans for Higher Education

—————

Before taking out a loan for your education, be sure to conduct thorough research and establish a clear repayment strategy.

Attaining a college or graduate degree can expand your career prospects and earning potential, but it may come with a significant price tag. When contemplating taking out a loan for education, it is important to weigh your choices, aim to borrow the minimum amount necessary, and devise and well-defined repayment strategy. Here are some guidelines to keep in mind.

• Obtaining a Student Loan •

To reduce your reliance on loans, begin by exploring your eligibility for scholarships and grants. Many students qualify for financial aid, so the first step is to complete the Free Application for Federal Student Aid (FAFSA), which can be accessed on the U.S. Department of Education's website at www.studentaid.gov[1]. This site also provides additional information on the FAFSA and grant opportunities.

• Know how much you need to borrow and make sure you can make the monthly payments •

To determine the amount you might need to borrow, subtract your estimated expenses (such as tuition, textbooks, housing,

---

1. http://www.studentaid.gov

food, and transportation) from your available resources, including savings, family contributions, work-study or job earnings, and scholarships or grants. Remember, your goal should be to keep your loan amount as low as possible, even if you qualify for a larger loan, as borrowing more will increase the amount you owe in the long run.

It is also important to take into account the minimum monthly repayment amount you'll need to make after graduation to pay off your loans, including interest. Make sure it corresponds to your projected income upon completing your studies. To estimate your future earnings in your desired fields, consult the U.S. Department of Labor's comprehensive wage statistics for more than 800 occupations at www.bls.gov/oes[2]. Your monthly loan payments will also depend on the interest rate and the term of your loan, which can range from 10 to more than 20 years.

While most student loans don't require monthly payments until after graduation, typically within six to nine months, it's crucial to understand that student loan debt is a significant commitment, warns Policy Analysts at the FDIC. Borrowing more than you can afford to repay can result in serious financial difficulties that persist long after graduation. It's important to note that unlike some other types of loans, federal and private student loans cannot be discharged through bankruptcy. Failure to repay your student loans may lead to referral to debt collection agencies, a negative impact on your credit score, which can result in higher credit costs and potential employment difficulties, as well as wage garnishment.

---

2. http://www.bls.gov/oes

If you require guidance on determining the appropriate loan amount, you may wish to consult a professional at your educational institution, such as a school counselor at your high school or a financial aid or admissions officer at your college. Additionally, a college budget calculator can be a useful tool, and you can access one from the Department of Education by visiting http://go.usa.gov/YhFC[3] and clicking on "Manage Your Spending."

• If you need to borrow, first consider federal loans •

It's important to remember that borrowing money for education is a serious financial decision that requires careful planning and consideration. By researching your options, minimizing your loan amount, and establishing a clear repayment plan, you can make informed decisions that will set you up for success after graduation. Utilizing resources such as college budget calculators and consulting with school professionals can also help you make sound financial choices. By taking these steps, you can help ensure that your education is an investment in your future, rather than a burden of debt.

Things to Do When You Are in School

• Set up direct deposit for your student aid money •

When receiving part of your student loan or financial aid, it's important to evaluate all options carefully, including any school-preferred products, which may have high fees and inconvenient ATM locations. Remember that you can deposit federal loan

---

3. http://go.usa.gov/YhFC

proceeds into any account you choose, giving you more flexibility and control over your finances.

• Keep track of the total amount you have borrowed and consider reducing it, if possible •

Reducing the amount you owe later on is possible through two strategies. If your loan accrues interest while in school, consider making interest payments during this period. Additionally, repaying some of the principal before the official repayment period begins can also help.

Paying Off Your Loan

• Choose a repayment plan •

Federal loans offer various repayment options, and you can switch to a different plan whenever necessary. For instance, one repayment plan starts with low monthly payments that gradually increase over time, while another is the "Pay as You Earn" program, which is set to be introduced by the Department of Education. This program allows you to pay 10 percent of your discretionary income (determined by the Department's regulations and usually the amount left over after essential expenses) every month. Moreover, you may be eligible for loan forgiveness if any remaining balance is present after 20 years of payments. In contrast, private loans typically require fixed monthly payments for a specified duration.

Federal loans may offer specific loan forgiveness benefits if you choose a career in public service. However, it's crucial to remember that the longer you take to repay your loan, the more interest you will pay (although you may be eligible for a tax benefit for the interest paid).

• Make your loan payments on time •

According to Senior Policy Analysts in the FDIC's Division of Depositor and Consumer Protection, student loans are usually reported to credit bureaus, so it's important to pay on time to establish a positive credit history. Conversely, late payments can harm your credit score. To ensure timely payments, you may wish to consider automatic deductions from your bank account or setting up email or text-message reminders.

To prevent missing important communication, such as changes to due dates, it's essential to ensure that your loan servicer, the organization responsible for collecting payments and administering your loan, has your current contact information.

• Consider making extra payments to pay down your loan faster •

To minimize your student loan debt, consider paying off the loans with the highest interest rates first. If you have multiple loans from the same servicer, specify that extra payments should be applied to the higher-rate loans. Refinancing could also be an option to obtain a lower interest rate and consolidate same-type loans into one. However, if you refinance or consolidate a federal loan into a private loan, you may forfeit crucial benefits, such as public service loan forgiveness. It's critical to contact your loan servicer immediately if you encounter difficulty repaying. According to the Deputy Director in the FDIC's Division of Depositor and Consumer Protection, borrowers of federal and private student loans may be eligible for assistance programs during challenging economic periods.

Learn more at www.studentaid.ed.gov.

Loans for Cars

———

Before considering purchasing a car, especially if you plan on borrowing money, it's crucial to consider the steps needed to comfortably afford it. While many young individuals look forward to having their own vehicle, there are important strategies to keep in mind before going to the dealership.

• Start saving early •

According to FDIC Community Affairs Specialists, providing a larger down payment on a vehicle purchase can minimize the amount you need to borrow, thus reducing the interest paid on a loan.

• Decide how much you can afford to spend each month on a car •

When considering a vehicle purchase, it's crucial to account for additional expenses such as insurance, taxes, registration fees, routine maintenance, and unexpected repairs. Online calculators can assist in determining affordability.

• Remember that there are alternatives to buying a car •

While lease payments may seem lower than loan payments, keep in mind that at the end of the lease, you won't own the car and could be responsible for additional expenses such as excess mileage or body repairs. If you only require a car occasionally, consider renting a vehicle through a service that offers hourly rentals.

• Shop for a loan at your bank as well as several other lenders •

When comparing loan options, it's important to examine the Annual Percentage Rate (APR) provided by each lender. The APR accounts for the overall cost of the loan, including interest and certain fees, as an annual rate. To expedite the process once you find a vehicle you like, consider getting pre-qualified by the lender that offers the most favorable deal. This isn't the same as loan approval, but it can streamline the process.

Prior to searching for a loan, review your credit report to ensure that inaccurate information is corrected, potentially qualifying you for a lower interest rate. While a dealer's special financing, such as zero-percent interest, may appear enticing, it may not be the most advantageous option if it means relinquishing an extra discount on the car. In such instances, obtaining a loan from a financial institution, even at a higher interest rate, may be more beneficial and save you money on the purchase price. It's also crucial to avoid purchasing a vehicle that is more expensive than you can afford, even if you're eligible for a larger loan.

• Whether you are buying or leasing, negotiate with the dealer based on the total cost of the car, not the monthly payment •

Extending the length of the loan enables dealers to offer a more costly vehicle with the same monthly payment as a less expensive vehicle, increasing the interest expenses paid over time.

Credit Cards: Avoiding Mistakes

———

C redit cards can be a helpful tool for establishing credit and making purchases, especially when you're starting out on your own. However, using them improperly can harm your credit score and lead to costly mistakes. The following tips can help you use credit cards responsibly.

• Read the fine print •

It's crucial to read and understand all the terms and conditions before applying for a credit card. This is particularly important when it comes to credit cards with low introductory interest rates, as you'll need to know when the introductory rate ends and what the new, higher rate will be.

• You can avoid fees by being aware of your card's credit limit •

FDIC Consumer Affairs Specialists advise that to avoid fees from going over your credit limit, it's better not to ask for the service that permits transactions over your limit. Instead, allow the transactions to be turned down, and you won't have to pay the fees.

• Try to pay the entire balance in full and on time every month •

Paying the balance in full can help you avoid interest charges and save money, but if you can't, aim to pay at least the minimum monthly payment amount and do so before the due date. Keep in mind that late payments can lead to fees and negatively affect your credit score.

• Think twice before applying for more credit cards •

Promotions like low introductory rates or discounts may entice you to apply for more credit cards. However, remember that every application will show up on your credit report as an inquiry, and multiple inquiries or new cards opened within a short period can lower your credit score. This scenario could indicate that you may be taking on more debt than you can manage.

• Take advantage of automated alerts from your card issuer •

Consider checking with your credit card issuer to see if it offers alert services that can notify you via cell phone or email of payment reminders, balance notifications if you're close to your credit limit, and information on suspicious activity that may indicate fraud. Additionally, find out if there are any associated fees for these services.

Dealing with Debt

———

For those struggling with debt, there are ways to take back control, regardless of age or circumstance.

• If you think you won't be able to make a loan or bill payment, contact the lender or others you owe •

Businesses and lenders may offer assistance programs to customers who are having difficulty making their payments. Waiting too long to seek help may result in penalties, late fees, and increased interest rates. Borrowers who wait until their accounts are past due may also miss out on possible options available to help them.

If you're struggling to make your mortgage payment, it's important to contact your lender or loan servicer as soon as possible to avoid defaulting on the loan and potentially losing your home. For more information on options to help you stay in your home, check out the FDIC's foreclosure prevention toolkit atwww.fdic.gov/consumers/loans/prevention/toolkit.html[1].

• Consider getting assistance from a reputable, nonprofit housing counselor (for rent or mortgage difficulties) or a credit counselor (for other debt) •

Consider seeking the help of a counselor if you have difficulty paying your bills or anticipate such challenges in the future. "Be cautious of paying a fee because nonprofit organizations offer

---

1. http://www.fdic.gov/consumers/loans/prevention/toolkit.html

this assistance at low cost or for free," advises Evelyn Manley, a Senior Consumer Affairs Specialist at the FDIC.

• Be on guard against scams •

Some scam artists promise loan approvals or debt settlement for less than what is owed, but then charge high upfront fees without providing any assistance.

• Remember that you have rights •

Debt collectors are required to follow certain rules and regulations when trying to collect a debt from you. Under federal and state laws, you are entitled to fair treatment and protection from harassment by debt collectors.

Consider checking out the Federal Trade Commission's resources for reliable assistance and ways to overcome a variety of debt problems at www.ftc.gov/bcp/menus/consumer/credit/debt.shtm[2].

---

2. http://www.ftc.gov/bcp/menus/consumer/credit/debt.shtm

Building Good Credit

———

Building a strong credit history is important for obtaining good interest rates on loans and other financial products, as well as for securing employment and housing. As you take on debts, such as credit card balances, rent, and loans, you are establishing a credit history. Credit bureaus compile this information into a credit score, which reflects your credit-worthiness. To maintain a good credit history, it is important to make timely payments and avoid carrying high levels of debt.

• Pay your loans, bills and other debts on time •

A good way to build and maintain a good credit history is to make sure you pay your loans, bills, and other debts on time. This will demonstrate that you are responsible with your finances.

• If you have a credit card, try to charge only what you can afford to pay off immediately or very soon •

If you can't pay your credit card bill in full, consider paying more than the minimum balance to reduce interest payments. Additionally, if you owe a large amount on your credit card compared to its credit limit, your credit score may decrease. Applying for multiple cards may also lower your credit score.

• Review your credit reports for errors •

You can improve your credit report and score by correcting any wrong information in your credit history. Obtain a free copy of your credit report from each of the three major credit bureaus by visitingwww.annualcreditreport.com[1] or calling toll-free 1-877-322-8228. If you can't resolve a dispute with a credit bureau regarding incorrect information on your report, you can submit a complaint online atwww.consumerfinance.gov/complaint[2].

Part 2: Saving Money

Consider setting up an automatic deposit from your paycheck to a savings account, so you won't even miss the money. Even a small amount deposited regularly can add up over time. Also, consider signing up for a retirement savings plan, such as a 401(k) if offered by your employer, and contribute enough to receive the full employer match if available. You may also want to consider investing in a low-cost index fund, which offers diversification and can help spread risk over multiple companies. By starting early and staying disciplined, you can gradually build a nest egg for your future needs.

• Save for specific goals •

It's important to have a savings plan for anticipated large expenses such as education costs, a home or car purchase, starting a small business, or preparing for retirement. For young adults just starting to be responsible for their own expenses, it's recommended to build an emergency fund that covers at least six months of living expenses to help during difficult times, such as a job loss or unexpected medical expenses not covered by insurance.

• Commit to saving money regularly •

Saving money regularly and earning compound interest can have a significant impact on your finances, even if you don't have a high income or a steady source of income. This is especially important when you are supporting yourself financially. Luke W. Reynolds, The FDIC's Division of Depositor and Consumer Protection emphasizes the importance of consistently adding to your savings and taking advantage of compounding interest to achieve long-term financial goals.

Try to set aside at least 10% of your income or any money you receive as savings. This is often referred to as "paying yourself first" because you are prioritizing saving over spending.

• Put your savings on auto-pilot •

Consider using automatic savings tools, such as round-up apps or automatic transfers from checking to savings accounts, to make saving money even easier. These tools can help you save small amounts of money that can add up over time.

• Make use of tax-advantaged retirement accounts and matching funds •

Consider exploring all your retirement savings options available at your workplace, which may come with employer matching contributions. Starting early in your career can help you take advantage of compound growth and retirement savings may hardly reduce your take-home pay due to income tax savings.

Consider opening an IRA (Individual Retirement Account) with a financial institution or investment firm and making regular transfers into it if you've contributed the maximum at work or if your employer doesn't offer a retirement savings program. You can also establish automatic transfers from a checking account to savings or investments for retirement or any purpose.

• Decide where to keep the money intended for certain purposes •

Here are some tips to help you organize your savings:

- Keep emergency savings in a separate federally insured savings account instead of a checking account to resist the temptation to use the funds for everyday expenses. Plan to replenish any withdrawals from your emergency fund.

- For large purchases you anticipate making in the future, consider certificates of deposit and U.S. Savings Bonds. They earn more interest than basic savings accounts because you agree to keep the funds untouched for a minimum period of time.

- Consider supplementing insured deposits with low-fee, diversified mutual funds or similar investments that are not deposits and are not insured against loss by the FDIC for long-term savings, including retirement savings. Keep in mind that you assume the risk of loss for the opportunity to have a higher rate of return over many years.

- Look into 529 plans for future college expenses, as they provide an easy way to save for college expenses and may offer tax benefits.

- Find out whether you are eligible for a health savings account, a tax-advantaged way for people enrolled in high-deductible health insurance plans to save for medical expenses.

• <u>Think about ways to cut your expenses and add more to savings</u> •

To reduce your financial expenses, start by researching lower-cost checking accounts at your bank or competitors. If you're paying interest on credit cards or fees for overdrafts, create a plan to stop this behavior. Analyze your monthly expenses, including food, utilities, and phone bills, to determine where you can save money.

For additional money-saving tips, visit www.mymoney.gov[1].

---

1. http://www.mymoney.gov

Choosing Banks

———

Choosing the Best Account for Everyday Banking

If you're a young adult starting out in your career or family life, or still in school, having a checking or transaction account is crucial for managing your finances. To make the most of this account and avoid unnecessary fees or expenses, consider the following tips.

> • Look for a bank account that offers low fees and the services you want •

Consider contacting multiple financial institutions to determine which accounts are most suitable for young adults or students. Examine the services you're most likely to use, as well as the associated fees, including any penalties for balances that fall below a certain threshold. Direct deposit of your paycheck is one service that you should expect to use. FDIC Consumer Affairs Specialists advise– when utilizing direct deposit, getting to the bank is no longer a concern because deposits are automatic. Direct deposit can be quick and may save you money.

> • Consider a low-cost banking account before settling for a prepaid card •

While reloadable prepaid cards can be a convenient option for some, they typically lack the comprehensive consumer protections, deposit insurance, and flexibility of a well-managed, low-cost insured deposit account. When selecting a financial account, it's important to consider the monthly charges, transaction fees, and benefits offered by each option. Insured deposit accounts offer greater safety and convenience for conducting a wide range of everyday banking transactions.

Consumer Affairs Specialists at the FDIC advise to review the cardholder agreement, which should be easily accessible on the prepaid card's website, before obtaining a reloadable prepaid card. This will ensure that you fully comprehend the terms and fees associated with the card.

It's important to understand that the funds you load onto a prepaid card may not be covered by FDIC insurance if the bank holding the money were to fail. Therefore, it's essential to read the cardholder agreement, which should be available on the card's website, and understand the terms and fees associated with the card. If you have any questions or concerns, you can call the FDIC at 1-877-ASK-FDIC (1-877-275-3342).

 • Debit cards provide a great service, but understand the pros, cons and costs •

FDIC Consumer Affairs Specialists suggest that debit cards can be an effective way to stay within your budget, provided you avoid overdrawing your account. As debit cards deduct funds directly from your checking or savings account, they can help you avoid borrowing money that you don't have.

Debit cards can offer a convenient and budget-friendly way to pay for purchases and access cash, but it's important to be aware of potential fees. Dropping below a minimum required account balance or using the card at another bank's ATM can result in charges. Additionally, lost or stolen cards should be reported immediately to minimize liability for unauthorized transactions. To avoid disruptions, it's a good idea to ask for speedy delivery of a replacement card if you rely on your debit card for all your transactions.

• Avoid overdraft costs •

This can help you keep track of your spending and avoid overdraft fees. Additionally, be aware that some banks may automatically enroll you in overdraft protection programs, which can be helpful in some situations, but can also lead to costly fees if you don't understand how they work. Be sure to review the terms and fees associated with any overdraft protection program before agreeing to enroll.

In recent years, federal regulations have required banks to obtain customers' consent before automatically enrolling them in overdraft programs for debit card purchases and ATM withdrawals. If you do not opt in and don't have enough funds in your account to cover a transaction, the transaction will be declined. While this may be embarrassing, it may be less costly than agreeing to the overdraft program. Check with your bank to learn about its overdraft policies, including any fees and ways to avoid them.

When deciding whether or not to opt in to an overdraft program, it's important to remember that the decision only applies to everyday debit card transactions. If you write a check when you don't have enough money in your account to cover it, the bank could still charge a significant fee. It's essential to carefully review the terms and conditions of any overdraft program before making a decision.

You can also avoid unexpected fees by keeping a close watch on your balance before spending money from your checking account. This can be easily done through online banking, mobile banking apps or by checking your account balance at an ATM.

If you receive an overdraft fee that you think is incorrect, promptly contact your bank. If the bank does not provide a refund, seek assistance from its federal regulator. If unsure of the regulator, file a complaint with the FDIC and it will be directed to the appropriate agency for investigation. Complaints can be submitted online at www2.fdic.gov/StarsMail/index.asp.

• For college student on financial aid, do your due diligence before choosing an account and a debit card •

Prior to receiving financial aid, it's important to review the program offered by your school. Familiarize yourself with the product's terms before committing to use it to access your financial aid. It may be more advantageous to have the financial aid deposited into your existing bank account with a debit card if you plan to use it on campus.

Smartphone Banking

———

M anaging Money on the Go

Mobile banking is becoming increasingly popular as financial institutions now offer the option to use smartphones for banking activities such as checking account balances, transferring funds, and making payments. However, it is important to take necessary precautions while using mobile banking to maintain security and avoid any potential risks.

● Ask your bank about the mobile banking services and any entailed fees ●

With the advent of mobile banking, some financial institutions now offer features such as remote check deposit and person-to-person payments through smartphones. While these options can offer convenience and flexibility, it's important to exercise caution when using them. Additionally, many banks offer text alerts for low balances, overdrawn accounts, and suspicious activity to help consumers stay on top of their finances.

● Know the risks for unauthorized transactions ●

According to Senior Policy Analysts in the FDIC's Division of Depositor and Consumer Protection, even though the same consumer laws that apply to other banking transactions typically protect you, it is crucial to read the disclosures that your bank provides about unauthorized transactions liability and comprehend the terms that apply to your transactions.

- As with all activities conducted online, be mindful of security

●

It is important to protect your mobile device with a strong password to prevent unauthorized access. Avoid lending your smartphone to others and have a plan in place in case it is lost or stolen, such as remote deletion of personal information. Be vigilant in monitoring your account for any unauthorized transactions or suspicious activity and report them immediately. Remember to take precautions not just for your online account, but for your mobile device as well.

Part 3: Scams and Thefts

• Best Practices for Young Adults to Avoid Fraud and Protect Privacy •

As fraudsters become more sophisticated, it's increasingly important to take precautions against identity theft. Anyone can be targeted, and it's essential to protect yourself against financial losses and the potential misuse of your sensitive information. If you're a young adult who spends a lot of time online, here are some general precautions to keep in mind.

• Use Internet passwords that are difficult to guess •

Consider using strong passwords with unique combinations of upper and lower-case letters, numbers, and symbols, and make sure to update them frequently.

• Never provide personal information whether in response to an unsolicited text message, e-mail, call or letter asking you to update or confirm personal information •

It is important to remember that banks will never contact you to confirm your bank account number or password as they already have this information. If you receive an unsolicited request for bank account information and are unsure of what to do, always contact your bank directly to verify its authenticity.

• Beware of an incoming e-mail or text message that asks you to click on a link •

Malicious software, also known as "malware," may be installed on your computer or mobile device by fraudsters to spy on you and gain access to your online banking sites.

• Be careful when sharing information on social networking sites •

The FDIC's Cyber Fraud and Financial Crimes Section warns that fraud artists can use social networking sites to gather personal information about you, such as your date of birth, your mother's maiden name, and family names that can help them figure out your passwords. These criminals may also pretend to be your friends or relatives and trick you into sending money or divulging personal information.

To avoid fraud on social media platforms, check your privacy settings and limit access to your personal information. The Internet Crime Complaint Center provides recommendations on how to avoid fraud on social media sites, and you can find them atwww.ic3.gov/media/2009/091001.aspx[1].

• Assume that any offer that seems too good to be true is most likely too good to be true •

Scammers frequently disguise themselves as charitable organizations or entrepreneurs promising awards, job offers, or other "opportunities." If you're feeling pressured to make a rushed decision and asked to send money or provide bank account information before receiving anything in return, exercise caution.

• Watch out for fraudulent checks or electronic money transfers •

A common scam involves receiving a check for more than you're owed from strangers or unfamiliar companies and being asked

---

1. http://www.ic3.gov/media/2009/091001.aspx

to wire back the difference. If the check is fraudulent, you could lose a significant amount of money. Be wary of such transactions and only deal with reputable individuals and companies.

• Protect your mail •

Consider using a paperless option for your financial statements, so they are sent to your email instead of your physical address. If you do receive paper statements, shred them before disposing of them. Also, be cautious of unsolicited emails or phone calls that ask for personal information. It is best to confirm the legitimacy of the request before sharing any information.

• Review all bank statements and credit card bills •

Notify your financial institution immediately of any irregularity or suspicious activity, such as an unauthorized withdrawal or charge, in your account.

• Keep your personal financial information safe •

It is important to keep bank and credit card statements, tax returns, old credit and debit cards, and blank checks out of sight. Make sure to shred these sensitive documents before disposing of them, as a dishonest roommate, relative, neighbor or any individual with access to your home might use them to commit identity theft or other crimes.

• Review your credit reports to ensure an identity thief hasn't obtained your credit card information or a loan in your name •

To ensure your credit reports are accurate and up-to-date, request a free copy from each of the three major credit bureaus.

Experts recommend spreading out the requests throughout the year. You can obtain a copy of your credit report by visitingwww.annualcreditreport.com[2] or calling toll-free at 1-877-322-8228.

Bonus: Tips for Teens

Saving and Managing Your Own Money

As a teenager, you begin to take on more responsibility for managing your finances and deciding how to save and spend your money. Here are some helpful tips to simplify and improve your decision-making.

• Consider a part-time work or a summer job •

Consider getting a job for extra income, as it can also provide valuable skills and connections for the future. When filling out a job application, it is generally safe to provide your date of birth and Social Security number for a background check if applying to a company with a local office. Ensure you hand the application to the manager if applying in person, and use the company's legitimate website if applying online.

The FDIC's Cyber Fraud and Financial Crimes Section advises being cautious of online job applications for part-time, work-from-home jobs offered by unfamiliar companies without a local office, as they may be attempting to commit identity theft rather than hire you.

• Deposit money in a savings account with specific goals in mind •

Community Affairs Specialists at the FDIC suggest setting both short-term and long-term financial goals such as college expenses. Start saving by depositing at least 10% of your income in a savings account as soon as possible. This approach, known as "paying yourself first," helps you resist spending temptations. Additionally, consider cutting back on expenses to increase your savings. Remember, the money you spend now could be needed for future goals or emergencies.

• Choose a checking account carefully •

According to the FDIC's Division of Depositor and Consumer Protection, while many banks offer accounts for students that require less money to open and charge lower fees, it's important to consider how you'll use the account and compare it to what other institutions offer.

Consider carefully before opting in to a bank overdraft program, as it may charge you a high fee of up to $40 for each overdraft transaction. Opting in could lead to a costly cycle of overdrafts. If you don't opt in, your transactions will be declined, but you can avoid penalty fees.

Consider arranging with your bank to automatically transfer money from a savings account to cover purchases if you don't have enough funds in your checking account. This may incur a fee, but it will likely be less than an overdraft fee.

• Understand the potential drawbacks of using a prepaid card •

Compared to credit or debit cards, prepaid cards may not provide the same federal consumer protections in case of loss or theft. Additionally, although they may advertise no monthly fees, they may still have charges for withdrawals, balance inquiries, and adding funds to the card. As such, it may be more beneficial to opt for a well-managed checking account for everyday transactions and easy transfers to a savings account.

• Keep a close eye on your bank account •

One way to avoid overdraft fees is to monitor your balance closely. Keeping track of receipts and expenses can help ensure that you do not spend more money than you have in your account.

• Actively take precautions against identity theft •

Be wary of any requests for personal information such as your name, Social Security number, passwords, or bank/credit card details, even if you don't have a credit card. Criminals may use your identity to access money or purchase goods. To avoid falling victim, do not provide any personal information unless you have initiated contact and verified the legitimacy of the request.

• Fully understand the cost and responsibility implications of borrowing money •

When borrowing money, compare offers based on the Annual Percentage Rate (APR) and consider that the longer it takes to repay the debt, the more interest you will pay. Missed loan payments can result in fees and difficulty securing affordable loans in the future.

Visit www.mymoney.gov[1], a U.S. government website that provides resources on personal finances from various federal entities, including the FDIC. The resources are organized by major life events, and there is a special section dedicated to young people.

---

1. http://www.mymoney.gov/

Bonus: Tips for Parents and Caregivers

P roviding Financial Aid: Saving for a Child's Future

As a parent or guardian, you may want to establish a solid financial foundation for the younger generation, and you may remember the difficulty of paying down student loans or other debt on a starting salary. Here are some ways to help your child financially.

• Plan and save for college expenses as early as possible •

According to the FDIC's Division of Depositor and Consumer Protection, it's best to start saving for your child's education as early as possible, even before they can speak. You can set up automatic transfers from your bank account or paycheck to a college savings fund, and online calculators can help you determine how much you need to save.

There are various methods to save for education, some of which offer tax benefits based on income and other factors. These methods include Section 529 college savings plans, U.S. Savings Bonds, traditional and Roth IRAs, Coverdell Education Savings Accounts, and accounts created under UGMA or UTMA. It is advisable to consult a tax advisor for guidance.

• Diversity savings and investments •

Consider different investment options for your savings, including FDIC-insured certificates of deposit and non-FDIC-insured options like mutual funds.

• Exercise caution when taking out a loan for the benefit of a child •

Before taking out a loan for education, it's important to make full use of all available free student aid, such as scholarships or grants. This can make it easier to repay the loan, reduce the amount of interest paid, and avoid the stress of a large student loan debt that can limit future opportunities.

Community Affairs Specialists at the FDIC stress the importance of considering the risks before co-signing a loan with a child since you will be responsible for paying the debt if the co-signer does not pay.

• Maintain life and disability insurance •

These can avoid financial ruin for your family and provide an extra cushion of support for higher education payments if something bad were to happen to you.

• Helping children open their very first bank accounts •

The FDIC's Outreach and Program Development Section recommends comparing key aspects such as minimum balance requirements and Annual Percentage Yield (APY) among several local financial institutions. This can help guide your child in selecting the right account for their needs. Some banks also offer special savings accounts for students with features like waived fees and a low minimum-balance requirement.

• Encourage saving money for future goals •

Encourage your child to set money aside for both short-term and long-term goals. Short-term savings can be used for fun activities like buying concert tickets or for emergency situations such as car repairs. Suggest putting at least 10% of any earnings or gifts into savings and consider matching their contributions as an incentive.

• Consider providing an allowance... even to a young adult •

Encouraging children to plan and decide how much they should save, spend, and set aside for sharing with others can help them develop a good financial system. It is essential to teach them the concept of "paying yourself first" before spending money.

FDIC Community Affairs Specialists suggest that an allowance is one of the best ways to teach children about money management and the trade-offs we face in life. To reinforce financial lessons, avoid giving extra money if they run out of their allowance early. Encourage your child to get a part-time or summer job once they're old enough.

• Set a good example with your own personal finance management •

Consider teaching your child the importance of monitoring their account transactions, such as their debit card, ATM, and other transactions. Explain how this helps them keep track of their current balance and avoid costly overdraft fees.

• Teach your kids to develop a healthy skepticism of unsolicited offers and inquiries •

Identity theft can happen to anyone, including young consumers and even babies. It is essential to protect children's personal information from scammers and identity thieves. The Federal Trade Commission's webpage on children's privacy offers information and tips for parents to safeguard their children's information from identity theft (www.ftc.gov/bcp/menus/consumer/data/child.shtm[1]).

• Discuss money with young people •

The FDIC's Division of Depositor and Consumer Protection suggest using any opportunity to engage in a conversation about financial choices and decisions with children. They recommend teaching children how to critically analyze ads because special offers may not be the great deal they appear to be.

---

1. http://www.ftc.gov/bcp/menus/consumer/data/child.shtm

Glossary

Accrued interest

the amount of interest that has accumulated on a loan or investment since the last interest payment or transaction date

Amortization

The process of gradually paying off a debt or loan over a fixed period of time, through regular payments that cover both the principal amount borrowed and the interest accrued

Annual percentage rate (APR)

A standardized calculation that expresses the annual cost of borrowing money, including interest rates and other related fees, as a percentage of the total amount borrowed

Appreciation

An increase in the value of an asset over time, due to market factors or other influences, such as improvements made to the asset or changes in supply and demand

Asset

Something of value that is owned by an individual, company, or other entity, and that is expected to provide economic benefit over time

Auto debit

A payment system in which a specified amount of money is automatically deducted from a bank account or credit card on a regular basis, to cover bills or other expenses

Balance

The amount of money or other assets remaining in a bank account or other financial account, after all withdrawals, fees, and other transactions have been accounted for

Balance sheet

A financial statement that provides an overview of a company's financial position at a given point in time, including assets, liabilities, and equity

Bankruptcy

A legal process for individuals or businesses that cannot repay their debts to creditors. It involves filing a petition with a court, which may discharge certain debts and restructure the repayment of others

Beneficiary

A person or entity named in a legal document such as a will, trust, or life insurance policy to receive assets or benefits upon the death of the owner of the assets

Budget

A financial plan that outlines income and expenses for a specific period of time, often monthly or annually. A budget can help individuals or businesses manage their finances and prioritize their spending

Capital

Refers to the financial resources that a business or individual has available to invest or use to generate income. It can include assets such as cash, property, and investments

Cash flow

The amount of cash that is generated or used by a business or individual during a specific period of time. Positive cash flow means more cash is coming in than going out, while negative cash flow means more cash is going out than coming in

Certificate of deposit (CD)

A type of savings account that typically offers a higher interest rate than a regular savings account in exchange for a fixed term commitment to keep the funds deposited in the account

Collateral

Assets pledged as security for a loan or other debt. If the borrower defaults on the loan, the lender may take possession of the collateral to recover their losses

Common stock

A type of ownership in a corporation that gives shareholders voting rights and the potential to receive dividends or capital gains based on the performance of the company

Compound interest

Interest that is calculated not only on the principal amount of a loan or investment, but also on any accumulated interest from previous periods. This can result in significant growth of an investment or increase in debt over time

Credit

The ability to borrow money or obtain goods or services with the understanding that payment will be made in the future. It can also refer to a person's creditworthiness, which is evaluated based on factors such as credit history, income, and debt-to-income ratio

Credit card

A payment card that allows the cardholder to borrow funds from a financial institution to make purchases, with the understanding that interest will be charged on any unpaid balance

Credit report

A record of an individual's credit history, including information about credit accounts, payment history, and outstanding debts. Credit reports are used by lenders and other entities to evaluate a person's creditworthiness

Credit reporting company

A company that collects and maintains information about individuals' credit histories and produces credit reports that can be used by lenders, employers, and other entities to evaluate credit-worthiness

Credit score

A numerical rating that represents an individual's creditworthiness, based on factors such as payment history, outstanding debts, length of credit history, and types of credit used. Credit scores are used by lenders to evaluate the risk of lending to a particular borrower

Credit union

A non-profit financial institution that is owned and controlled by its members, who typically share a common bond such as living or working in the same area. Credit unions offer many of the same financial services as banks, including savings and checking accounts, loans, and credit cards

Creditor

A person or entity that is owed money by another person or entity, typically in the form of a loan or other debt

Debit

An accounting entry that represents the amount of funds or assets that a person or company owes

Debit card

A payment card that allows the cardholder to access their funds directly from their bank account to make purchases or withdraw cash from an ATM

Debt

An amount of money borrowed by one party from another, with the agreement to repay the borrowed amount plus interest over a predetermined period of time

Debt service

The payment of interest and principal on a loan or debt over time

Deductible

The amount of money an individual or business must pay before an insurance policy will cover the remaining costs associated with a loss or damage

Delinquency

Failure to make payments on a debt or loan according to the agreed-upon terms

Direct deposit

The electronic transfer of funds directly into a bank account, usually by an employer or government agency as payment for wages, salaries, or benefits

Diversification

The practice of spreading investments across different asset classes, such as stocks, bonds, and real estate, in order to manage risk and maximize return

Dividend

A payment made by a corporation to its shareholders as a portion of its earnings

Equity

The value of an asset minus any debts or liabilities owed on that asset

Face value

The nominal value assigned to a financial instrument, such as a bond or a stock, that is stated on the instrument itself

Fair market value

The estimated price at which a property or asset would be sold in a transaction between a willing buyer and seller, both of whom are knowledgeable about the asset and the market conditions.

Federal Deposit Insurance Corp. (FDIC)

A U.S. government agency that provides insurance to protect depositors against the loss of their deposits in case a bank or savings institution fails

Finance charge

The total cost of credit, including interest and any other fees, that a borrower must pay on a loan or line of credit

Finance company

A business that specializes in providing loans to individuals or businesses, typically at higher interest rates than traditional banks

Financing fee

A fee charged by a lender for providing financing or credit to a borrower

Flexible spending account

A tax-advantaged savings account that allows an individual to set aside a portion of their pre-tax earnings to pay for qualified medical expenses or dependent care expenses

Foreclosure

The legal process by which a lender seizes and sells a property when a borrower is unable to repay their mortgage or loan

401(k) plan

A retirement savings plan sponsored by an employer, in which employees can make pre-tax contributions from their salary, and employers may also contribute to the account on behalf of the employee

Health savings account (HSA)

A tax-advantaged savings account that can be used to pay for eligible medical expenses for individuals with high-deductible health plans

High-deductible health plan (HDHP)

A type of health insurance plan that requires a higher deductible than traditional plans, but typically has lower monthly premiums

Home warranty

A contract that covers the cost of repairs or replacement of certain home appliances and systems for a specific period of time

Individual development account (IDA)

A savings account designed to help low-income individuals build assets through matched savings for specific goals such as home-ownership or education

Individual retirement account (IRA)

A tax-advantaged retirement savings account that individuals can contribute to each year up to a certain limit

Inflation

The rate at which the general level of prices for goods and services is increasing, resulting in a decrease in purchasing power over time.

Installment plan

A payment plan that allows a borrower to repay a debt over time through a series of regular payments

Insurance premium

The amount of money an individual or business pays for an insurance policy to provide coverage for a specified period of time

Interest

The cost of borrowing money, usually expressed as a percentage of the amount borrowed

Interest rate

The rate at which interest is charged on a loan or earned on an investment, expressed as a percentage of the amount borrowed or invested

Investment

The act of committing money or capital to an asset with the expectation of obtaining additional income or profit in the future

Investor

A person or entity who commits capital with the expectation of obtaining additional income or profit in the future, usually through investments in stocks, bonds, or other assets

Leverage

The use of borrowed money to invest in assets, with the aim of increasing the potential return on investment. It can amplify gains, but also magnify losses

Liability

In accounting, a liability is an obligation or debt that a company or individual owes to others. It can refer to a financial or legal obligation, such as a loan, tax bill, or accounts payable

Liability

In personal finance, liability refers to any legal or financial obligation that one owes to another party, such as a debt, mortgage, or lease agreement

Lien

A legal claim on property or assets that serves as collateral for a debt. It gives the creditor the right to sell the property or assets to satisfy the debt if the borrower fails to repay

Liquidity

The ability to easily convert an asset into cash without losing value. Assets that are highly liquid can be quickly and easily sold or traded, while illiquid assets may take longer to convert to cash and may lose value in the process

Load

A sales charge or commission that is added to the cost of an investment product, such as a mutual fund or insurance policy. It can be a one-time charge or a recurring fee

Loan

A sum of money borrowed from a lender with the expectation of repayment, usually with interest, over a specified period of time. Loans can be secured or unsecured, and can be used for various purposes such as buying a home, starting a business, or financing education

Management fee

A fee charged by an investment manager or financial advisor for managing a client's assets. It is typically a percentage of the assets under management

Market value

The current price or value of an asset in the market, based on supply and demand. It can fluctuate based on various factors, including economic conditions, company performance, and investor sentiment

Maturity

The date on which a debt or investment becomes due for payment or redemption. For example, the maturity date of a bond is the date on which the bond issuer must repay the principal to the bondholder

Money market account

A type of savings account that typically offers higher interest rates than traditional savings accounts, but with more restrictions on withdrawals. It may require a higher minimum balance and may limit the number of transactions per month

Mortgage

A loan used to purchase a home or other real estate, secured by the property itself. The borrower makes regular payments over a specified period of time, typically with interest, until the loan is fully repaid

Municipal bond

A debt security issued by a state or local government to finance public projects or services, such as schools, hospitals, or infrastructure. Interest on municipal bonds is generally exempt from federal income taxes and may be exempt from state and local taxes as well

Mutual fund

An investment vehicle that pools money from multiple investors to purchase a diversified portfolio of securities, such as stocks, bonds, or other assets

Net worth

The difference between an individual's total assets and total liabilities. It is a measure of an individual's financial health and can be used to evaluate financial progress over time

Par value

The face value of a security, such as a bond or stock, as indicated on the certificate. It is often different from the market value of the security

Payday loan

A type of short-term loan that typically has high fees and interest rates and is meant to be repaid with the borrower's next paycheck. Payday loans are often considered predatory lending because they can trap borrowers in a cycle of debt

Predatory lending

Lending practices that take advantage of vulnerable borrowers, such as those with poor credit or low income, by charging excessive fees or interest rates, or by offering loans with terms that are difficult to understand or meet

Prepaid debit card

A card that is loaded with funds in advance and can be used to make purchases or withdraw cash. Unlike credit or debit cards, prepaid cards are not linked to a bank account and do not require a credit check

Pretax

Refers to income, contributions, or expenses that are not subject to taxation. For example, contributions to a 401(k) plan are often made on a pretax basis, which means that they are not taxed until they are withdrawn

Prime rate

The interest rate that commercial banks charge their most creditworthy customers for loans. The prime rate is often used as a benchmark for other interest rates, such as those on credit cards or mortgages

Principal

The original amount of a loan or investment, before interest or other charges are added.

Promissory note

A legal document that outlines the terms of a loan, including the amount borrowed, interest rate, repayment terms, and any collateral that is required. It serves as a binding agreement between the borrower and the lender

Qualified plan

A retirement plan that meets certain requirements set by the Internal Revenue Service (IRS) and offers tax advantages to both the employer and the employee. Examples include 401(k) plans and traditional pensions

Return

The gain or loss on an investment over a specific period of time, expressed as a percentage of the original investment amount. It can refer to the interest earned on a savings account, the dividends paid on a stock, or the appreciation in value of a real estate investment, among other things

Revenue bond

A type of municipal bond that is issued to finance public projects, such as highways, bridges, or public buildings. The bond is backed by the revenue generated by the project, rather than the full faith and credit of the issuer

Risk

The possibility of loss or damage, particularly in relation to an investment. It is often measured in terms of volatility or variability of returns, and can be influenced by factors such as market conditions, economic trends, and company-specific risks

Roth IRA

A type of individual retirement account that allows individuals to contribute after-tax dollars and withdraw funds tax-free in retirement. It is often used as a retirement savings vehicle for those who expect to be in a higher tax bracket in retirement than they are currently

Savings account

A deposit account held at a bank or other financial institution that earns interest on the balance

Secured credit card

A type of credit card that requires a security deposit to be held by the issuer as collateral for the credit line

Stock option

A contract that gives the holder the right, but not the obligation, to buy or sell a specific stock at a predetermined price within a specified period of time

Stockholder or shareholder

A person or entity that owns shares of stock in a company

Tax-deferred

Refers to an investment or account in which taxes on earnings or contributions are deferred until a later date, such as retirement

Term

The length of time until a debt or investment reaches maturity or is due

Terms

The conditions and requirements of a financial agreement, such as a loan or credit card

Treasury bond

A debt security issued by the U.S. government with a fixed interest rate and a maturity of more than 10 years

Treasury Inflation-Protected Security (TIPS)

A bond issued by the U.S. government that provides protection against inflation by adjusting the principal value of the bond based on changes in the Consumer Price Index

Treasury note

A debt security issued by the U.S. government with a fixed interest rate and a maturity of between one and 10 years

U.S. savings bond

A debt security issued by the U.S. government that pays interest and has a maturity of up to 30 years

Utilization rate

The percentage of a credit limit that is being used at any given time

Also by Matthew Green

Guide to Modern Personal Finance
Guide to Modern Personal Finance: For Students and Young Adults

34931748R00042